Date Due

1999	– – 2005				
2001	DEC 19 20				
002	DEC 27				
SEP 28	DEC 1 4 2011				
OCT 26	1/7/15				
2003	12-22-15				
DEC 16	12-10-16				
2004					
DEC 30					

A WORLD OF HOLIDAYS

Christmas

A WORLD OF HOLIDAYS

Christmas

Catherine Chambers

RSVP
RAINTREE
STECK-VAUGHN
P U B L I S H E R S
The Steck-Vaughn Company

Austin, Texas

Published by Raintree Steck-Vaughn Publishers, an imprint of Steck-Vaughn Company

Library of Congress Cataloging-in-Publication Data

Chambers, Catherine.
    Christmas / Catherine Chambers.
        p.   cm. — (A world of holidays)
    Includes bibliographical references and index.
    Summary: Examines the traditions and celebrations associated with the holiday of Christmas.
    ISBN 0-8172-4608-8 (hardcover)
    ISBN 0-8172-8104-5 (softcover)
    1. Christmas—Juvenile literature.   [1. Christmas.}
I. Title.   II. Series.
GT4985.5.C43   1997   1|17|02
394.2'663—dc20   96-33583
                                         CIP   AC

Printed in Spain
Bound in the United States
2 3 4 5 6 7 8 9 0 02 01 00 99

ACKNOWLEDGMENTS

Editor: Su Swallow, Pam Wells
Design: Neil Sayer
Production: Jenny Mulvanny

For permission to reproduce copyright material, the author and publishers gratefully acknowledge the following:

Cover: Andrew Ward/Life File
Title page: James Davis Travel Photography
Contents page: Zefa **page 6** Circa Photo Library/John Fryer **page 7** (top) Zefa, (bottom) Jennie Woodcock, Reflections Photo Library **page 8** Garo Nalbandian/Robert Harding Picture Library **page 9** Andrew Ward/Life File **page 10** (top) Zefa, (bottom) Chris Bland/Eye Ubiquitous **page 11** Hans Reinhard/Bruce Coleman **page 12** (top) trip/V Kolpakov, (bottom) Collections/Geoff Howard **page 13** Circa Photo Library **page 14** (top) Romilly Lockyer/Image Bank, (bottom) James Davis Travel Photography **page 15** Ellen Rooney/Robert Harding Picture Library **page 16** Robert Harding Picture Library **page 17** (top) Zefa, (bottom) Trip/H Rogers **page 18** Private Collection/Bridgeman Art Library **page 19** (top left) Trip/H Rogers, (top right) David Hurn/Magnum, (bottom) H. Gruyaert/Magnum **page 20** (top) Zefa, (bottom) Jennie Woodcock/Reflections Photo Library **page 21** Mayer-Magnum **page 22** (top) Trip/A Tjagny-Rjadno (bottom) Food Features **page 23** Robert Harding Picture Library **page 24** Gerard Champlong/Image Bank **page 25** (left) Blair Seitz/Photo Researchers, Inc. (right) Alan Becker/Image Bank **page 26** Hermitage, St. Petersburg/Bridgeman Art Library **page 27** (left) Nigel Sitwell/Life File, (right) Micha bar Am/Magnum **page 28/29** Alan Towse Photography

Contents

The Meaning of Christmas

Christmas! It means so many things. For Christians all over the world, it celebrates the birth of Christ. For others, it is a chance to show caring and giving. Long ago, winter parties brightened the dark days and honored the sun.

CHRISTMAS BEGINNINGS

The dazzling color and light of Christmas celebrate the birth of just one baby, Jesus Christ. He was born over 2,000 years ago in today's West Bank. But Jesus was no ordinary baby. When he grew up, his life and teachings were so powerful that people wanted to follow them. These people were called Christians.

A manger scene shows Jesus Christ and Mary, his mother. Shepherds and the three kings kneel to worship him.

Angels and a Christmas tree light up New York's Rockefeller Center.

It's fun decorating the Christmas tree with shiny balls.

IN THE BLEAK MIDWINTER

The Christian Church only decided to celebrate Chrismas about 350 years after Jesus was born. No one really knows exactly when his birthday was. But Christmas has always been celebrated in either December or January. This fit in well with ancient winter festivals in North Africa and Europe. Ceremonies were held to make the sun shine again in the spring and to bring good harvests.

When is the special day? Before Jesus was born, some people celebrated the birth of a different holy baby. It was the Persian god, Mithra, born on December 25. This is the day when most Christians now celebrate Christmas. So perhaps the two festivals were joined together. Other Christians in parts of Europe celebrate on January 6. Some Armenians wait until January 17!

Caring and giving were a normal part of many winter festivals. And there's someone who fits in well with this tradition. Yes, it's Santa Claus!

7

The Christmas Story

The Bible is one of many ancient books about God. It was written in this book that one day, a special baby would be born, bringing joy and light to the world. His name was Jesus.

This is the town of Bethlehem, where Jesus Christ was born. You can see the hills where the shepherds watched over their sheep.

After Jesus was born, Mary and Joseph had to flee from King Herod. Mary and Jesus were carried on a donkey.

THE NEWBORN KING

About 2,000 years ago, a carpenter called Joseph and his wife, Mary, had been chosen by God to have this special baby. They both knew this was true, because angels had told them so.

At that time, there was a mean ruler in Palestine called King Herod. Just before Jesus was born, the king ordered all the people in the land to go back to the place where they had been born. There, they would all be counted. So Joseph took Mary with him on a long journey to his birthplace, a small town called Bethlehem. Mary felt really tired when they got there. She knew that the baby would soon be born. Joseph tried to find them a place to stay, but all the small inns were full. Hundreds of people had come to be counted.

Joseph was getting desperate. There was no room anywhere. Finally he found a kind innkeeper who showed them to the only room he had—a stable, carved out of rock. Inside, there was an ox and an ass, lots of straw, and not much else. It was here in this poor stable that Jesus Christ was born.

SHEPHERDS AND KINGS COME TO WORSHIP

That night on the chilly hills around Bethlehem, shepherds were looking after their sheep. It seemed like any other night, until a flash of light blinded them. When they could see clearly, the shepherds saw an angel. He told them to leave their sheep and follow the bright star that shone over the stable. There, they would find the Son of God. When the shepherds got there, they knelt down at the feet of Jesus.

Later, three kings, often called the Magi or wise men, arrived from the East. They came to worship the new great king and offered rich gifts to the baby Jesus.

9

A Glow in Winter

The early leaders of the Christian Church in Rome wanted people to accept the new Christian customs. But they let people keep their old festivals, or holidays, too. It made the people feel much happier about being Christians.

Winter holidays were held in cold, snowy villages—like this one in Norway.

THE OLD AND THE NEW

The Romans helped to spread Christianity as they marched through their huge empire—from the Middle East to as far west as Ireland. But they brought other religious customs, too. And it was all right to take part in a mixture of customs.

Romans celebrated the sun in winter. They often carved pictures of the sun. People have made sun carvings ever since—like this one on a sundial.

The Romans wanted a warm sun and rich harvests in the year to come. So during winter, they held a seven-day feast to honor Saturn. He was the god of farming. He kept everyone well fed. At the feast, candles were lit. People gave each other presents and little dolls made of clay or pastry. Green-leaved branches were cut to be used for decoration. These are like some of our Christmas customs today.

Wherever the Romans went, they discovered that other people had winter holidays, too. In Great Britain and northern France, they found that the Celts held a winter celebration. We get the tradition of kissing under the mistletoe from the Celts. What a mixture our Christmas traditions are!

Mistletoe invites kisses at Christmas. It usually grows on apple trees.

Carols, Chimes, and Pantomimes

From carol singers to bell ringers, music has been an important part of Christmas for hundreds of years. Plays and pantomimes are important, too.

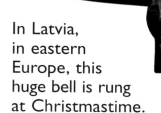

In Latvia, in eastern Europe, this huge bell is rung at Christmastime.

SINGING IN A CIRCLE

Handbells and church bells are rung at Christmas to mark the birth of Christ. But what about the Christmas carol?

Long ago in many parts of Europe, carols were just songs that were sung by people standing in a circle. They were sung at all kinds of festivals and holidays.

A few hundred years after the birth of Christ, special carols were written for Christmas. They were not like the dull, church hymns of

Choirboys singing Christmas carols in London's Westminster Abbey.

the time, written in Latin. Latin was a language that few people understood. Carols were songs for ordinary people, written in their own language. The songs were simple and joyful, and people could sing them anywhere, not just in church.

About 500 years ago, some very strict Christians, the Puritans, stopped people from singing carols. Carols sounded too happy! For 200 years, there were only a few parts of Europe where people dared to sing them. But the tradition survived, especially in parts of France, Germany, and Great Britain. Now they are written and sung by Christians in all corners of the world.

MIMING AND RHYMING

There's plenty of entertainment at Christmastime. Many people perform nativity plays about Mary and Joseph's journey to Bethlehem. Long ago, all over the Christian world, people performed miracle plays, which were about the Christmas story. But they also staged folktales. The actors, known as mummers, wore strange costumes and mimed and danced the stories. In England about 200 years ago, the plays were spoken in rhyme. Later, they turned into what is known today as pantomime!

A nativity play is acted by schoolchildren. In the back row, you can see shepherds, the angel, and the three kings.

13

The Holly and the Ivy

Gingerbread, cookies, trees, glass balls, and paper chains are all well-known Christmas decorations. Long ago, houses were draped with holly, ivy, and mistletoe.

MISTLETOE MYSTERY

In ancient midwinter festivals, people draped holly, ivy, and evergreen boughs around their houses and over each other, too! They believed it would bring back the sun. But mistletoe was probably the most special decoration of all. Its clusters of pale green berries, like little lights, would surely make the sun shine? But for Christians, mistletoe was too closely connected with these old religions. You probably will not see mistletoe in churches today.

Holly and ivy decorate this manger scene.

A BABY, LYING IN A MANGER

If you open a church door at Christmastime, you are almost sure to see a stable scene, glowing in the dim light. With models of Joseph, Mary, the baby lying in a manger, and the shepherds, it reminds people of what Christmas means to them. These models became part of the Christian Christmas in 1224, when

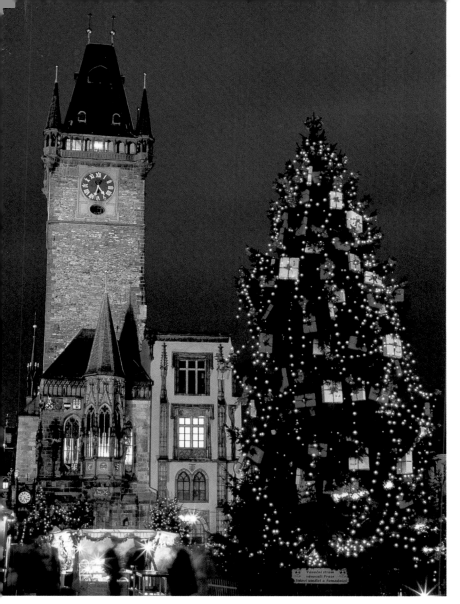

A Christmas tree in Prague, in the Czech Republic, covered in tiny white lights. Some people put a star at the top of the tree. Others put a doll or an angel there instead.

Saint Francis of Assisi made the first nativity scene. He loved all the animals. So you will find an ox and an ass in the stable, too.

OH, CHRISTMAS TREE! OH, CHRISTMAS TREE!

The biggest decoration of all is probably the Christmas tree. This custom started in the German Black Forest. Here, the dark evergreen trees grow so thickly over the hillsides that they look like a black forest. The tradition spread through the rest of Germany and Europe about 200 years ago. German settlers took it to America, too. Today, you can see Christmas trees in all corners of the world, though many are made of plastic! But what do these trees strung with lights mean? Some say that the dark green leaves are the night sky, and the tinsel and lights are the stars.

15

Calendars and Crowns

Christmas is coming! In churches all over the world, Christians prepare for the religious celebration. Stores are full of people buying presents!

READY, SET, GO!

You can probably find Christmas presents in the stores as early as October. Lights and decorations glow in the streets starting in November. But the Christian Church does not start to get ready for Christmas until the fourth Sunday before December 25, the big day for most people.

This time of preparation is called Advent. It means "the coming," and began more than 1,500 years ago. Advent is celebrated on the last four Sundays before Christmas.

The Church wanted Christians to see the birth of Christ as a light shining in a world of darkness.

So on the first Sunday of Advent, darkened churches held very sad,

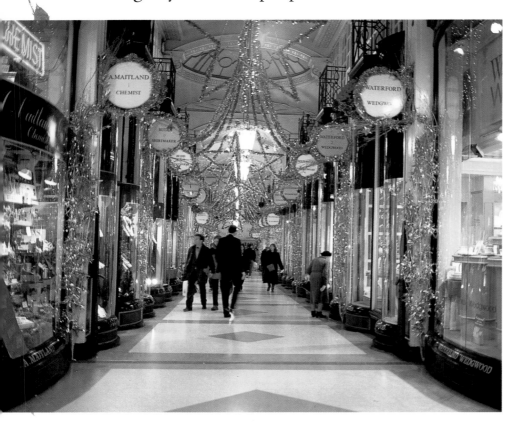

Christmas shoppers search the store windows for presents to buy.

This church in Jerusalem is dark during Advent.

solemn services. They got a little bit brighter and more cheerful on the next Sunday, and so on. On Christmas Day, joy and light shone in every church!

ON THE NIGHT BEFORE CHRISTMAS

Carol singing and party games, kissing under the mistletoe, and midnight mass are all part of Christmas Eve. This is how people in many parts of the world celebrate. Each country has its own traditions, along with the ones that most of us share. In southern Portugal, plates are piled high with crisp, sticky pastries. Families gather, and presents are handed out. For here, Christmas Eve is the main celebration. In Denmark, people fast, eating only rice. Italians serve fish dishes. There are so many different traditions!

During Advent today, children in many parts of the world open the first door of an Advent calendar on December 1 and the last door on Christmas Eve.

This child is opening her Advent calendar.

Santa Claus Is Coming!

On this card from the 1800s, Father Christmas is weighed down with presents.

Who is Santa Claus, or Father Christmas? How does he fit into the Christmas holiday? The mystery began hundreds of years ago and in many different places!

GIVING AND CARING

Some people say that the first Santa Claus came from Carthage in North Africa. He was a greedy god who gobbled up all his presents, which were. . . children! I don't think I'd leave out a peanut butter and jelly sandwich for him! Others say that he was the Roman god, Saturn, or even the Viking god, Odin. Perhaps he started off as one of the green fairy gods with horns on their heads. They came from many different parts of Europe. All these gods were kind and generous at wintertime, when people held festivals to honor them.

The Christmas story fits in well with these ancient traditions of giving. The shepherds and later, the three kings, offered gifts to Jesus.

A picture of St. Nicholas in a Greek Orthodox church.

Children in Switzerland join a St. Nicholas parade.

JINGLE BELLS!

The name Santa Claus really comes from "Saint Nicholas." Nicholas lived on the Greek island of Myra, 1,600 years ago. He was a kind bishop. He gave money to a poor family and, it is said, helped sailors by calming stormy seas.

Nicholas became famous for his good deeds. After he died, the Church made him into a saint. The feast day of Saint Nicholas was first celebrated only on December 6. But this secret giver of presents later became part of Christmas goodness and excitement!

People from Holland took the idea to the United States and made the character we know today. At first, he was dressed in green—the green of kind winter spirits from ages past. But over 100 years ago in America, a cartoonist called Nast drew him with a bright red robe. Santa Claus had arrived!

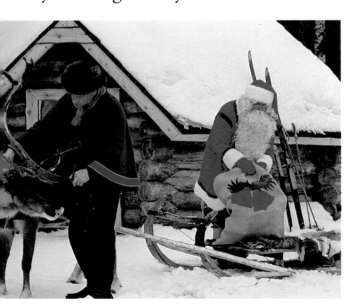

In Finland, Father Christmas loads his reindeer sleigh.

A Merry Christmas!

Christmas Day in a sleepy snow-covered village or on a hot sandy beach—how do people all over the world celebrate? And what happens in Bethlehem, the very birthplace of Jesus Christ?

Father Christmas arrives in a surfers' rescue boat in Sydney, Australia.

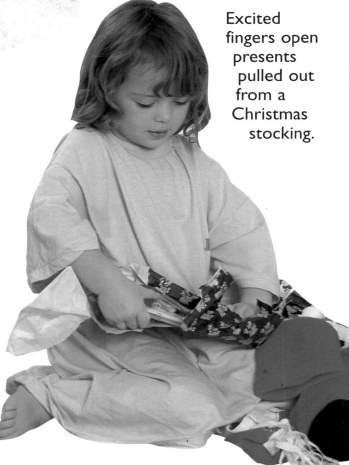

Excited fingers open presents pulled out from a Christmas stocking.

THE WORLD AT CHRISTMAS

It's December 25—Christmas Day for most Christians throughout the world. Some have already celebrated Christmas the night before. So today is a time for rest and for thinking about what Christmas really means to them.

For others, whether in frosty air or hot sunlight, there is much excitement. Families and friends gather. Presents are opened. The church, shining with lights, opens its doors. In cold climates at home, a feast is laid out on the table. In hot climates, it is spread out on a picnic cloth!

But what of Bethlehem, where it all started so long ago? The birthplace of Jesus is marked on the floor of a lamp-lit cave with a silver star. Over that cave is a church—the Church of the Nativity. At Christmastime, Christians flock here to see where their faith began.

It is believed that this star marks the spot where Jesus Christ was born. It is set in the floor of a cave in Bethlehem.

Outside is an open space called Nativity Square. Hymns and Christmas greetings blare out from loudspeakers to the crowds. There are lights and gift shops, the same as in any other place of great interest and importance.

21

Christmas Dinner

A Russian family enjoying a traditional Christmas dinner. Cheers!

At Christmas, people in different parts of the world have always eaten their special treats, from roast turkey to boiled turtle. They finish with colorful cakes and fruit puddings and pies.

MEAT TREATS

Tastes for Christmas meat dishes have changed over time. Turkey is now a great favorite in many parts of the world. But chicken is still the holiday dish in Africa and regions of South America. A hundred years ago, goose was the dish of the day. Early settlers in Canada enjoyed nothing better than a piece of boiled buffalo. And on an Australasian island, turtle was the thing to eat. Even farther back in time, rich people ate all sorts of exotic birds at Christmas—from guinea fowl to peacock.

Many of us also eat ham. Eating pork goes back to a time when pigs and wild boar were sacrificed to please the god of the sun. Pig killings and boar hunts still go on at this time in parts of Europe. In the far north of Europe, people make special Christmas cookies, in the shape of a pig!

CAKES, COOKIES, PIES, AND ALL THINGS NICE

In Germany, Christmas food fairs are held in many of the cities. Brightly lit stalls are piled high with spiced cakes and colored marzipans. In Spain and Italy, all kinds of nutty nougats are

Many people eat roast turkey at Christmas.

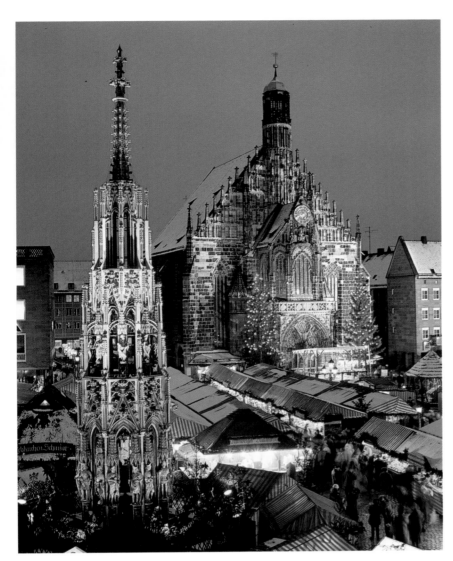

Sweet treats and cakes of all types are sold at this Christmas market in Nuremberg, Germany.

a Christmas treat. Nougat was brought to southern Europe by people of a very different faith—the Moors, Muslims from North Africa.

The Portuguese make huge round cakes with a hole in the center. They are decorated with plump, juicy limes, cherries, and plums. In the United States, steaming fruit and mincemeat pies are for dessert. Today mincemeat is dried fruit, but long ago it was really meat.

ON THE FEAST OF STEPHEN

It's the day after Christmas. Now everyone can relax. But it is also the Feast of Saint Stephen, the first Christian to die for his faith. For parts of Europe, it is also a time for hunting and riding horses. In England, it is Boxing Day. During Victorian times, servants were given boxes of gifts on the day after Christmas.

23

And a Happy New Year!

What could be more exciting than Christmas? For many people, New Year's Day on January 1 is the most important winter holiday. Long ago, darkness and evil were finally swept away at this time.

WHAT'S YOUR RESOLUTION?

Eight hundred years ago, many people celebrated Christmas at New Year. The birth of Christ and the birth of a hopeful new year were brought together. Many of the old New Year's customs have now been moved to Christmas Day, but making a resolution is a New Year tradition.

A New Year's resolution is a promise to do something good or to behave better for the whole year! This is the birth of something new in our own lives. But how long can you keep your resolution? It isn't easy.

In Paris, France, Christmas lights shine on into New Year.

DANCING IN THE STREETS

There are so many ways to celebrate New Year. On New Year's Eve in most of the world's capital cities, young people fill the squares. Sometimes they dance under freezing cold fountains! But there are older customs that still live on. In Philadelphia, mummers in amazing costumes play banjos as they parade through the streets. These actors mime scenes and folk stories from long ago. They clown around, too!

In Philadelphia, mummers dance through the streets to the sound of banjos.

KNOCKING ON THE DOOR AT MIDNIGHT

In Scotland, New Year's Eve is known as Hogmanay, which probably means "gift." Giving is part of the fun of the first-footing ceremony that takes place at the chimes of midnight on New Year's Eve. The first person to pass through the front door as the new year is rung in is given a special welcome. The first-footer knocks on the door and carries in gifts of food or coal!

Scottish bagpipes are played at Hogmanay.

The Coming of the Kings

Christmas ends on the Twelfth Day, January 6, with Epiphany. This reminds Christians how God showed himself to the world through Jesus Christ. It also marks the arrival of the three kings to Bethlehem.

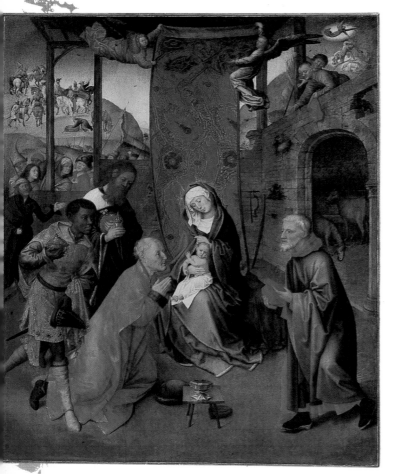

This picture of the three kings was painted more than 600 years ago.

GREAT KINGS BOW DOWN

This is the last part of our story. It tells of the journey of three kings to Bethlehem. They came from far-off lands, perhaps from the East and Africa. All of them knew from their studies that a great king, Jesus Christ, had just been born. So they set out to greet him, guided by the bright star that shone over the stable. But their journey was not a smooth one.

Do you remember mean King Herod from the first part of the Christmas story? Well, the kings stopped at his palace and told him of the newborn king. Herod was jealous and deeply alarmed. So he told the kings that when they found the baby, they should come back and tell him. Herod said that he wanted to greet the baby, but really he wanted to kill him!

The kings promised to return and went on their way to Bethlehem. There they knelt at Christ's feet and offered gifts of gold, sweet-smelling incense, and myrrh. Before they left, they were told in a dream to stay away from Herod. So the three kings returned home a different way, and the newborn baby was safe.

ON THE TWELFTH DAY OF CHRISTMAS

So it's the Twelfth Day of Christmas, and things are coming to an end. In many homes, this is when the last chocolate on the tree is eaten, and all the decorations come down. But in some parts of the world, the celebrations have only just begun! In parts of South America, people in bright costumes dance and parade in the streets. In Mexico, a rich Twelfth-Day cake is baked.

In Spain, it is believed that the three kings pass by every house to leave gifts. And the children leave out their shoes. They are filled with straw for those hungry camels that carried the three kings all the way to Bethlehem.

In Bethlehem, the Greek Orthodox Church holds its Christmas celebrations. They take place on January 6.

Young kings ride to the Festival of the Kings in Ecuador on January 6. This is Christmastime for people there.

Let's Celebrate!

You too can join in the celebrations. Try making this pop-up card and some New Year's poppers. You can get lots of ideas for decorating them by looking at the pictures in the book.

MAKING A CHRISTMAS CARD
Materials:

- cardboard or oaktag
- paints, felt-tip pens, or crayons
- safe scissors
- glue
- decorations such as glitter, sequins, and ribbons

Directions:

1. Fold the cardboard in half one way. Then fold it in half again, the other way. Look at the picture to help you.
2. Cut two slits on the inside of the card as shown in the picture. Then lift the strip of card so that it sticks out in a "seat shape."
3. Draw a picture on the front of the card. Or cut out one from wrapping paper or old Christmas cards. Then stick them to the card. Use lots of colorful decorations.
4. To make the inside pop-up: Make another picture on a separate piece of cardboard. Try to keep it a simple shape such as a holly leaf or a snowperson. Stick it onto the front part of the lifted "seat" shape strip of card.

Now your card will fold flat, and a picture will pop up when you open it!

MAKING NEW YEAR'S POPPERS

Materials:

- crepe paper and drawing paper
- an empty kitchen roll cut into three to make three poppers
- popper fillers such as candy, pencil sharpeners, erasers or balloons
- paints, felt-tip pens or crayons
- glue or paste
- decorations such as sequins and glitter

Directions:

1. Cut out the crepe paper and drawing paper as shown in the picture. You could paint a picture or write a joke on the drawing paper.
2. Place the popper filler inside the kitchen roll.
3. Roll the drawing paper around the kitchen roll. Glue the paper down lightly.
4. Roll all this in the crepe paper. Glue the crepe paper down. Now tuck the crepe paper into the holes of the drawing paper and kitchen roll. Leave some at the ends for pulling!
5. You can now decorate your popper brightly.

Glossary

Angel A messenger from God.

Bishop A senior priest in the Christian Church.

Celebrate To show that a certain day or event is special.

Ceremonies More solemn ways of celebrating a special day.

Fast To eat only certain foods, or nothing at all—often as part of a religious custom.

Hymn A religious song.

Manger An eating trough for animals such as oxen and asses.

Mummers Actors in folk plays.

Saint A good person, thought to be especially holy after he or she has died.

Spirits Beings that you can't see—something like ghosts.

Tradition A custom, a way of doing something passed down from parents.

Further Reading

Daniel, Becky. *Christmas Story.* Good Apple, 1990.

Delacre, Lulu. *Las Navidades: Popular Christmas Songs from Latin America.* Scholastic, 1990.

DePaola, Tomie. *The Family Christmas Tree Book.* Holiday, 1980.

Giblin, James C. *The Truth About Santa Claus,* HarperCollins Children's Books, 1985.

Goode, Diane. *Diane Goode's American Christmas.* Dutton Children's Books, 1990.

Langstaff, John. *What a Morning! The Christmas Story in Black Spirituals.* Simon and Schuster Childrens, 1987.

Lankford, Mary D. *Christmas Around the World.* Morrow, 1995.

Rollins, Charlemae H., ed. *Christmas Gif': An Anthology of Christmas Poems, Songs, and Stories Written by and About Black People.* Morrow Junior Books, 1993.

Index